Managing Credit

by Jennifer Boothroyd

Consultant: Kari Servais
Middle School Family & Consumer Science Educator

BEARPORT
PUBLISHING

Minneapolis, Minnesota

Credits

Cover and title page, © Kiwis/iStock; 4, © Pixel-Shot/Shutterstock; 5, © RossHelen/Shutterstock; 7, © Janon Stock/Shutterstock; 9T, © Drazen Zigic/Shutterstock; 9B, © Eric Broder Van Dyke/Shutterstock; 11, © ultramarine5/iStock; 13, © Andrey_Popov/Shutterstock; 15, © Rawpixel.com/Shutterstock; 17, © GaryPhoto/iStock; 19, © LUMPANG MOONMUANG/Shutterstock; 21T, © Standret/Shutterstock; 21B, © Leszek Glasner/Shutterstock; 23, © Kmpzzz/Shutterstock; 25, © Vgstockstudio/Shutterstock; 27, © Atstock Productions/iStock; 28TL, © jenny on the moon/Shutterstock; 28TR, © Colorlife/Shutterstock; and 28B, © VectorHot/Shutterstock.

Bearport Publishing Company Product Development Team

President: Jen Jenson; Director of Product Development: Spencer Brinker; Senior Editor: Allison Juda; Editor: Charly Haley; Associate Editor: Naomi Reich; Senior Designer: Colin O'Dea; Associate Designer: Elena Klinkner; Associate Designer: Kayla Eggert; Product Development Assistant: Anita Stasson

Library of Congress Cataloging-in-Publication Data

Names: Boothroyd, Jennifer, 1972- author.
Title: Managing credit / Jennifer Boothroyd.
Description: Silvertip books. | Minneapolis, Minnesota : Bearport Publishing Company, [2023] | Series: Personal finance: need to know | Includes bibliographical references and index.
Identifiers: LCCN 2022032852 (print) | LCCN 2022032853 (ebook) | ISBN 9798885094184 (library binding) | ISBN 9798885095402 (paperback) | ISBN 9798885096553 (ebook)
Subjects: LCSH: Consumer credit--Juvenile literature. | Finance, Personal--Juvenile literature. | Teenagers--Finance, Personal--Juvenile literature.
Classification: LCC HG3755 .B66 2023 (print) | LCC HG3755 (ebook) | DDC 332.7/43--dc23/eng/20220708
LC record available at https://lccn.loc.gov/2022032852
LC ebook record available at https://lccn.loc.gov/2022032853

For more information, write to Bearport Publishing, 5357 Penn Avenue South, Minneapolis, MN 55419.

Contents

Fast Money

You want ice cream, but you don't have any cash. There's the emergency **credit** card your parent gave you, but ice cream is not an emergency! When you use a credit card to buy something, that money needs to be paid back later. How can you be smart about using credit?

For most credit cards, you must be 18 years old to have your own **account**. Some places let younger people have cards that are connected to an adult's account.

What Is Credit?

Credit is money given out by a bank or company. It lets people buy things without spending their own money right away. However, people must eventually use their money to pay back the credit. Many people get credit through credit cards and **loans**.

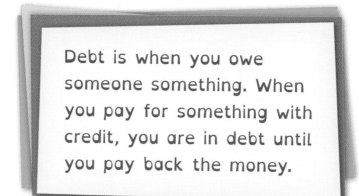

Debt is when you owe someone something. When you pay for something with credit, you are in debt until you pay back the money.

Borrowers and Lenders

People who use credit are called **borrowers**. These borrowers use credit for many reasons. Some want to buy things without spending cash, such as when they shop online. Credit also helps people make big purchases when they do not have enough money to pay for something all at once.

Businesses use credit, too. They may borrow money to pay for new buildings or to fix expensive equipment. Some may even use credit to pay their workers.

Someone may choose to pay for a new TV using credit.

A borrower gets credit from a **lender**. This is often a bank. There are also companies whose business is lending money.

When people borrow, they need to pay back more than they get. Lenders charge a fee for the opportunity to use their money. This extra money paid back is called **interest**.

Lenders do not always charge the same amount of interest. The amount may depend on how much money someone borrows. It can also depend on how long it will take the borrower to pay back the money.

Take a Chance on Me

Lenders don't give credit to just anyone. They want to be sure the borrower will pay it back. So, lenders look at how a person has used credit in the past. This history is shown through the person's credit score. The better a borrower's score, the more likely a lender will be to give them credit.

A credit score is a number. It often ranges from 300 to 850. A higher number is better. Someone with a good score has been responsible with credit in the past.

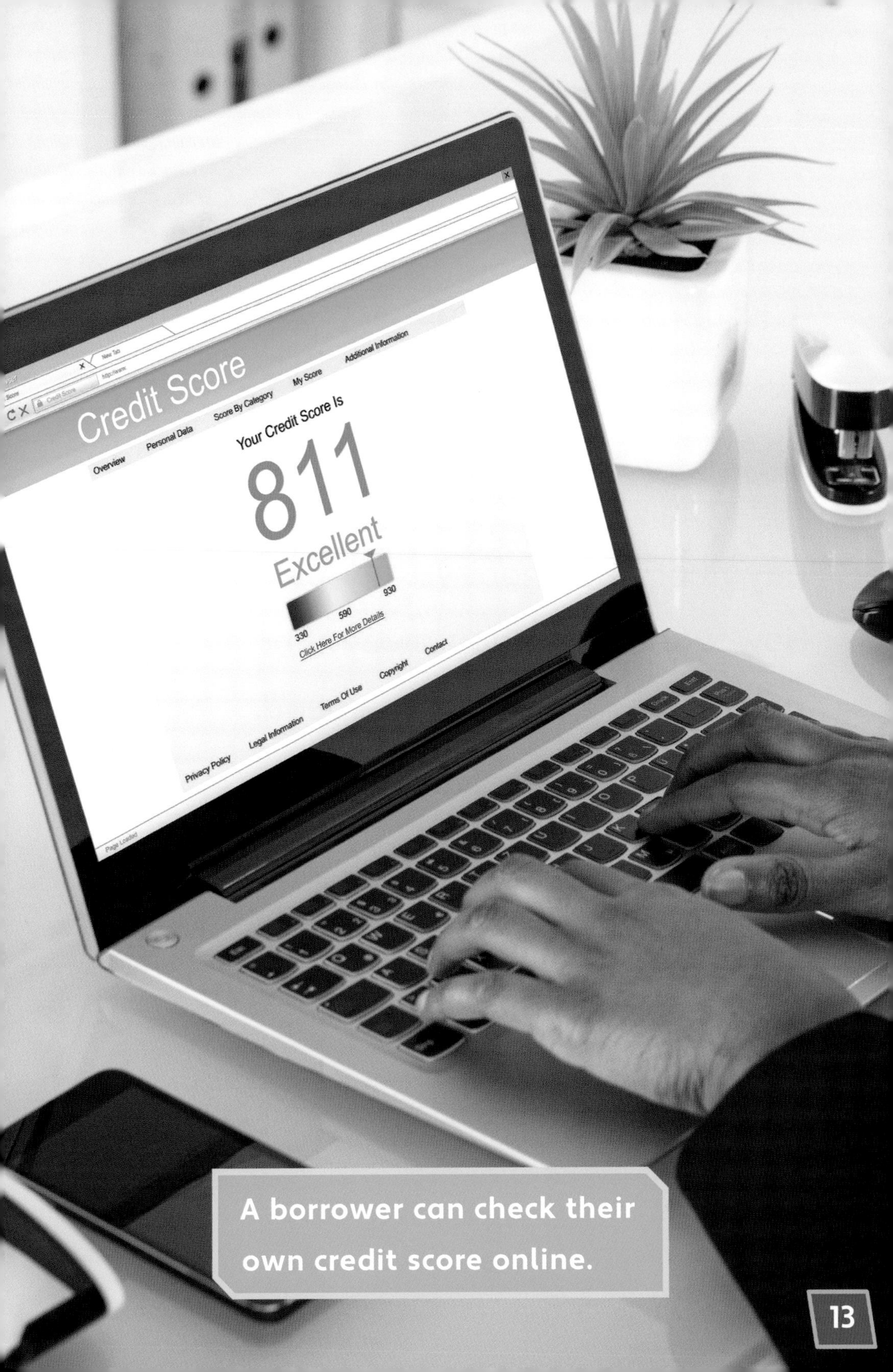

A borrower can check their own credit score online.

It Keeps Going

There are many kinds of credit. With a credit card, a borrower gets credit up to a certain amount. They can keep using the credit card as long as they make payments for money they borrowed. However, when they owe more money, they have less credit to spend.

The **maximum** amount of money a borrower can spend is called a credit limit. If someone reaches their limit, they won't have credit to use until they pay some back.

A credit card user does not have to pay back all the money at once. However, they must at least make regular **minimum** payments. A small part of the total is usually due every month. If a borrower misses these payments, they may lose their credit.

The amount owed on a credit card gathers interest. When more money is owed, more interest is due. Borrowers often try to make higher payments so they pay less interest.

Minimum Payment Due:

$20.00

New Balance:

$271.53

Late Payment Warn...

minimum payment by

have to pay a late fe...

...eased up to t...

For One Time Only

Another common type of credit is a loan for a specific purpose. Borrowers use this credit for only a certain length of time. Interest is added to the credit amount, and the total is split into payments. The account is closed after all the money is paid back.

Some loans have to be paid back within a few years. Others last 30 years or more. A borrower agrees to pay back their loan and its interest in that time.

People often get loans to purchase homes.

LOAN APPLICATION

Application is assessed individually. The...
This form may be posted with all the supporting do...
If submitting in person, please do so before 3.30pm

Your details:

...ame.........................
...of birth.........................
...phone number.........................

Loans help people pay for all kinds of expensive things, such as cars or home improvements. Why get a loan instead of using a credit card? Most credit cards do not offer enough credit for very large purchases. They also charge more interest.

A loan for buying a home is called a mortgage. A loan that pays for schooling after high school is called a student loan.

The Cost of Credit

Using credit almost always means paying more than just the money that was borrowed. Interest adds up. Until a borrower pays back everything they owe, their credit account will keep gathering interest. This means they will pay more the longer they take to pay the loan back.

Most credit cards have a short amount of time in which the borrower can pay back everything without interest. This is called a grace period.

Along with interest, most lenders also charge **fees**. There might be a fee to open a credit account. There are often fees for late payments.

Smart borrowers look at how much lenders charge in interest and fees before choosing credit. Finding the lowest costs could save them money.

Fees aren't the only downside of late credit payments. If a borrower does not make payments on time, it affects their credit score. This could make it harder for them to get credit in the future.

People can learn about different lenders online.

Using Credit Wisely

Credit can be very helpful. However, this easy way to pay can sometimes make people forget how much they are spending. Making smart choices about when and how to use credit can make managing money easier in the future.

A budget tracks how much money you get and how much you save or spend. This includes how you are using credit. Having a budget can help you make good decisions with money.

CREDIT CARD

Paying by Credit Card

Buying something with a credit card is simple. Making a payment can be just as easy. Here's how it all happens.

You use your card to buy something.

The credit card company pays for the purchase.

You send money to the company to pay them back.

The credit card company sends you a bill.

★ SilverTips for REVIEW

Review what you've learned. Use the text to help you.

Define key terms

borrower

credit

interest

lender

loan

Check for understanding

Describe one way people can use credit.

What is a borrower, and what is a lender?

How does interest change the amount you spend on something?

Think deeper

What are some reasons to use credit and some reasons not to use it?

★ SilverTips on TEST-TAKING

- **Make a study plan.** Ask your teacher what the test is going to cover. Then, set aside time to study a little bit every day.

- **Read all the questions carefully.** Be sure you know what is being asked.

- **Skip any questions** you don't know how to answer right away. Mark them and come back later if you have time.

Glossary

account an arrangement with a bank or company to hold, send, and receive money

borrowers people or businesses that use someone else's money and agree to pay it back

credit money given by a bank or company that must be paid back

fees money paid for extra services

interest extra money that is paid on borrowed money

lender a person or business that gives someone money and expects it to be paid back

loans one-time payments of money that must be paid back

maximum the largest possible amount

minimum the smallest possible amount

Read More

Fiedler, Heidi. *The Know-Nonsense Guide to Money: An Awesomely Fun Guide to the World of Finance! (Know Nonsense Series).* Mission Viejo, CA: Walter Foster Jr., 2022.

Gagne, Tammy. *Credit Cards and Loans (Money Basics).* San Diego, CA: BrightPoint Press, 2020.

Uhl, Xina M. and Ann Byers. *Getting a Credit Card (Managing Your Money and Finances).* New York: Rosen Publishing, 2020.

Learn More Online

1. Go to **www.factsurfer.com** or scan the QR code below.

2. Enter "**Managing Credit**" into the search box.

3. Click on the cover of this book to see a list of websites.

Index

About the Author

Jennifer Boothroyd's first credit card was for a clothing store. She learned the hard way to keep track of how much she was spending with her card. Since then, she has used credit carefully to pay for a car, a house, and her college tuition.